Raising Child Actors

15 Expert Tips for Raising Kids in Show Business

Every year, thousands of parents help their children pursue their dreams of becoming an actor. Success requires not only determination, but an understanding of how to deal with the many issues that families of aspiring young actors encounter throughout their career.

In this informative Itty Bitty Book, entertainment industry insider, Dr. Lima Bergmann, shows you what to expect and how to prepare your child, yourself and your family for the most common situations parents face during the different phases of a child actor's career.

- *"Lima has written a wonderful and easy to follow book of tips for parents of aspiring young actors. I wish this invaluable information had been available to me when my daughter began auditioning."* – Laura Klein, mother of Alisan Porter (former child actress and winner of Season 10 of *The Voice*)
- *"I wish I'd had this book as a guide when we moved to L.A. Many aspects of this business took me by surprise. This should be required reading for all families of child actors."* - Pam Bushman, mother of actress Lindsay Bushman.
- *Lima's personal and professional experience uniquely positions her to provide healthy, positive advice for families in the entertainment business. This Itty Bitty book is a text book for success."* - Toni Casala, Founder, Children In Film

Get a copy of this book today and gain the knowledge and the confidence needed to support your child actor.

Your Amazing Itty Bitty®
Raising Child Actors Book

15 Expert Tips for Raising Kids in Show Business

Lima Bergmann, PsyD

Published by Itty Bitty® Publishing
A subsidiary of S & P Productions, Inc.

Copyright © 2017 Lima Bergmann, PsyD

All rights reserved. No part of this book may be reproduced or transmitted in any form or by any means, electronic or mechanical, including photocopying, recording or by any information storage and retrieval system, without written permission of the publisher, except for inclusion of brief quotations in a review.

Printed in the United States of America

Itty Bitty® Publishing
311 Main Street, Suite D
El Segundo, CA 90245
(310) 640-8885

ISBN: 978-0-9987597-2-2

This book is dedicated to my soul mate, Reid. Life is never boring with you! For all the hard decisions we had to make together over the years, I couldn't be more pleased with the amazing experiences we've had and the way our family has blossomed. You are the glue…

To my lovely daughters, Lyndsy and Hannah, you are my angels from heaven. I don't know what I did to deserve to be your mother, but it is my absolute greatest pleasure in life. I marvel at both of you every day.

Thank you to all of the wonderful people who have supported and fostered my daughters' careers over the years: Diane Hill Hardin, Nora Eckstein, Judy Savage, Thom DeLorenzo, Patrick Day, Meredith Fine and Dana Fletcher, Wendi Green and Jennifer Millar.

I would also like to lovingly thank Chuck James, Dar Rollins, Lorrie Bartlett and ICM Partners; Lainie Sorkin-Becky, Nicole King and Management 360; Margot Menzel and Primary Wave Entertainment; Tyler Grasham and APA Agency; and Saxon Trainor, for all of your hard work in developing and promoting the talents of Lyndsy and Hannah.

Stop by our Itty Bitty® website to find additional information regarding raising child actors.

www.IttyBittyPublishing.com

Requests for private consultations, speaking events or interviews may be sent to:

DrLima@RaisingChildActors.com

Table of Contents

Introduction

Tip 1	Just for Starters
Tip 2	All For One and One For All
Tip 3	What About My Job?
Tip 4	Move It or Lose It
Tip 5	It Takes A Team
Tip 6	Reading, Writing and Arithmetic
Tip 7	Money, Money, Money
Tip 8	The Balancing Act
Tip 9	Staying Ahead of the Game
Tip 10	Just…Don't
Tip 11	"The Mom" / "The Dad"
Tip 12	Kids Will Be Kids
Tip 13	Fame
Tip 14	Behaviors On Set
Tip 15	On Their Own

Introduction

Congratulations and welcome to the entertainment business! This *Itty Bitty® Book* contains 15 expert tips regarding the most critical issues parents and their children face as they start their journey into the entertainment business. Each family's journey is unique and will involve many new personal and professional decisions, challenges and dynamics.

When my family first ventured into the entertainment business, there was no instruction book. The guiding principal was, "Go with your gut and hope for the best." Some of the most important lessons came the hard way!

This Itty Bitty® book offers you valuable universal advice and tips, from a mom and Clinical Psychologist, who for over fifteen years raised two daughters in "The Business." Included are tips for keeping your family's life on track and suggestions for keeping balance in your dual role as a parent *and* the person guiding your child's career. It's a business, and until your child is of age, you are not only a parent, but a CEO.

Whether you are thinking about taking the plunge, already have a toe in the water, or have been in the game for awhile, this book is for you. It's not a how-to book on getting your child into the business. It's about knowing what to expect and how to deal with things as a parent once you've made the decision to go forward.

This book is organized to take you from the first steps of the journey to the transition phase into young adulthood, as your actor[1] learns to take responsibility for their own career.

The tips are purposely concise to meet the abbreviated format of this book. If you would like to learn more, you can request a private consultation, speaking event or interview by contacting me at DrLima@RaisingChildActors.com

My husband and I are incredibly grateful for the amazing opportunities and experiences the entertainment industry has provided to our daughters throughout their childhoods and for all the wonderful people who have helped them along the way. They have grown into strong, healthy, independent and happy women. We wish you all the same blessings.

---

[1] For the purposes of this book, I refer to your child as "your actor" because, in the context of the profession, that's what he or she is. That being said, I don't recommend you ever refer to your child as "your actor" in real life!

Tip #1
Just for Starters

Here are just a few starting tips for the beginners. Like with any new business, you will have many things to learn, but with this one you have a young person's emotions to consider, as well.

1. You're giving your actor an incredible opportunity to pursue their passion. Along the way, be open to the excitement and adventure of the journey. Avoid becoming overly focused on the outcome.
2. You and your actor may encounter naysayers who will tell you that your actor is losing out on a "normal" childhood. IMO, "normal" is overrated.
3. Don't waste time comparing your actor's journey to anyone else's. No two paths unfold exactly the same.
4. There are exciting opportunities along the way that will require major decisions…but rarely include guarantees.
5. Your actor will develop important life skills and an education no classroom could ever provide.

The Craft:
- Acting is not only about booking a job. Your actor will learn about becoming the best they can be, honing their skills, auditioning, networking and working hard. Focus on the process with your actor so that getting a part isn't the only thing that defines their success.

Positivity:
- "You're crazy, you'll never succeed..." Model for your child that other's opinions should never stand in the way of their dreams.
- Teach your actor the 3 P's: Patience, Passion and Persistence.

Practical Skills Needed:
- Organization; Communication; Commuting wizardry; Researching; Quick, informed decision making; Money management.

Street Smarts:
- Do your research on the business of child acting. Know what you need and what you don't because scammers are on the lookout for blissfully ignorant parents.

Well-Rounded:
- With a proper attitude and your loving guidance, your actor will become bright, disciplined, skilled, flexible, open to diverse relationships, and respectful of others. These valuable qualities will serve them in any future profession.

Tip #2
All For One and One For All

There are family matters to consider.

1. At the outset, discuss with your partner how each of you can support your actor and how challenging decisions will be handled. A coordinated and unified approach is best.
2. Explain to siblings that compromises will be necessary, and what to expect if major changes are unavoidable. Their reactions may range from excitement to jealousy. Emphasize that the accomplishments and needs of all siblings will always remain equally valued.
3. It's called show "business." Agree together on the parameters of your business plan including the time, money and effort the family is willing to invest.
4. If, at any time, it's decided that this is not the path to continue on, be supportive and loving with your actor without any guilt trips. Don't ever convey disappointment or signal that they are responsible for sacrifices the family made on their behalf to pursue this career. Celebrate and appreciate all that you learned and shared together on the journey.

Communicate and Coordinate with Each Other.

- Decide with your partner who will do the day-to-day leg work with your actor and who will focus more on the home front. Extended family, friends and hired help can be immensely beneficial.
- Have regular family meetings. Make sure that everyone is heard, all needs are being met and no one is feeling overburdened or overlooked.
- Don't let unforeseen, last minute auditions or bookings create chaos and drama for the family. Be flexible and always have a reliable "Plan B" ready to implement for any surprises.
- Don't ever get so wrapped up in the business that you lose the ability to say "no." Know your actor's limits and you and your family's limits. Take a break if you need to refresh or regroup. It's called "booking out" and there is nothing wrong with it.
- Three years is adequate time to allow for training, plenty of auditions, feedback, and for casting directors to become familiar with your actor. At about this point, consult with your family and team to assess and reevaluate the plan going forward.

Tip #3
What About My Job?

Balancing your "day job" while supporting your actor's career can be a challenge. Here are some tips:

1. Think outside the box. A boss you think is inflexible might consider your request to work remotely or agree to flex hours if you present a reasonable plan.
2. After-school hours are the busiest time for your actor with auditions, acting classes, coaching, etc. A job that allows you to work during school hours is ideal.
3. A major challenge is when you're notified that your actor has booked a job and you have little-to-no notice to make arrangements. Pay attention to the shoot dates listed on audition appointments to prepare yourself in advance for potential conflicts with your work schedule.
4. A guardian is always required to be on set with your actor. If you or your spouse can't leave your jobs, someone else will need to accompany them. One option is to hire a "set sitter."

Employment Options:

- If you are a service provider, work during school hours, after 7pm or on Saturdays.
- If you have a partner, try working different days or shifts. Don't be ships passing in the night, though. Make sure you have plenty of time as a couple and as a family.
- Explore working remotely. Some jobs will allow you to do this, even if just temporarily. Ask for this ahead of time so if you decide to go to L.A. for pilot season, or if your child books a job, it won't be a surprise to your employer.
- Set sitters are an invaluable resource for working parents. Ask your team if they have any referrals. Confirm that they have experience and are professional and reliable. Consider getting a background check, including their driving record.
- Internet Marketing is growing and can be very profitable. You can work from your laptop almost anywhere.
    - Network Marketing - Pick a niche, choose a product and a company, find a consultant to sign with, then start your business.
    - Affiliate Marketing - sell other people's products and earn a commission.
    - Create your own digital information product and sell it online.

Tip #4
Move It or Lose It

It's not necessary to move to Los Angeles or New York right away to start an acting career.

1. Begin by building up your actor's resume with the opportunities in your own local market. Then, when ready, seek representation in a larger market.
2. When you find representation interested in your actor, they may ask if you're willing to move to a larger market location. The more available you are to them, the more auditions your actor will get submitted for. More auditions mean better odds of booking a job.
3. When your actor has representation, gets great feedback from auditions and has even booked a job or two, you're at a point where you might consider a move.
4. However, if the time is not right for your family, don't feel pressured to move. There are still other options.
5. Moving doesn't mean your actor's career is going to stay settled in one location. You could move to L.A. or N.Y., only to find a year later that your actor has booked a series regular role in Toronto… It happens all the time.

Options in Your Local Market:

- School plays, community theater, regional theater, college student films and theater (they cast younger people too) and local film productions.
- L.A. and N.Y. are busiest for auditioning, but shooting locations are widely spread and local talent hires are needed. Chicago, Louisiana, North Carolina, Texas, Vancouver, Toronto, Georgia, are just a few places with major productions.

Your Actor Has Representation But You're Not Ready To Move...

- Self-tape most auditions, but fly in for the big ones, such as testing for a series regular role. There is a real advantage to auditioning in person versus self-taping. However, self-tape auditions are becoming more common. Many great roles have been booked this way.
- Have one parent or family member make the move with your actor to L.A. for pilot season (roughly, January-April). It's a good chance to see how your actor takes to the business, what kind of feedback they get, and how the lifestyle feels. There are entire apartment complexes that cater to families who do this. Whether or not your actor books anything, this trial period will allow you to see how the business resonates with you and your actor.

Tip #5
It Takes A Team

Your actor's team can include agents, managers, publicists, acting coaches and lawyers. Research each person well before you interview them and check out their client list.

1. Be realistic about where your actor is in the hierarchy of talent so you can seek out representation that is a good match.
2. The process of interviewing can widely differ. Depending on the age and maturity level of your actor, you may or may not be asked to sit in on the interview. If you are, never speak for your actor. It's important for the interviewer to get to know your actor and how they present themselves.
3. Be clear about your boundaries for your actor. "No scary movie auditions, no leaving the state for a series role, no auditions during my actor's soccer season," etc…are issues to communicate at the start. It's a reality that the more limits you have, the more difficult it will be to find representation for your actor. However, your values must take precedence and if they don't align with particular roles or the lifestyle, you might realize that acting isn't a good fit.

Agents and Managers:

- Don't compare your actor's level of activity to others'. If you're reliable and your actor is getting decent feedback, trust that your team is submitting them for work. They want your actor to book as much as you do.
- CD's (Casting Directors) can't see everyone and oftentimes an actor isn't a good fit for a role. If you feel like your actor isn't getting out enough, check in with your team and politely ask if things have been slow for your actor's age group. There can be lulls from time to time for certain ages.
- Good communication with your team is important, but keep in mind that they have many clients to take care of. Ask for a meeting twice a year to let them see how your actor is maturing. Email is a good way to ask quick questions or provide updates about your actor.

Acting Coaches:

- Acting coaches can have a huge impact on your actor's success. Be tuned in to how your actor feels and behaves after a coaching session. If they are stressed or unhappy and not getting good audition feedback; the coach (even a good one) might not be the best fit for your actor.

Tip #6
Reading, Writing and Arithmetic

Here are some basic tips for school issues:

1. Auditions generally start after regular school hours. Get to school early to get in the front of the pick-up line and schedule your actor's easiest class for last period in case you have to pull them early.
2. Stock the car with school supplies for homework because you will be driving a lot in this business. When you are within thirty minutes of the casting office, switch your actor from homework to audition preparation mode.
3. When on set, there are very strict rules about school hours and work hours for professional actors. They are different for each age group, so get familiar with them.
4. Studio Teachers are very important people on set for your actor's education, general wellbeing and safety. Most are amazing, but not all (just like real life). Get a business card from anyone your actor resonates with because if they ever book a lead role, you might get to make a teacher request.

Schooling Options:

- Public School is fine until your actor starts working steadily. They don't allow frequent absences.
- Private Schools tend to be more flexible with absences for actors.
- Independent Study Programs (overseen by your public school district) are traditional schooling done at home, but often allow participation in activities such as dances or sports in the school.
- Private Independent Study Programs are online or correspondence schools with traditional school curriculum. The cost and quality will vary.
- Homeschooling is the most flexible option. Local homeschool groups are popular and typically rich with activities. Homeschooling is free but you need to buy your own curriculum.
  Homeschooling laws vary in each state.

School On Set:

- There should always be a studio teacher present when your actor arrives for work. Call your team if no one is there.
- Never go to a job, or even pre- or post-production work, without your actor's schoolwork. You'll be sent home.
- It's possible that your actor's school assignments don't all get completed. Make a list for the teacher that prioritizes them so the most important assignments are finished first.

Tip #7
Money, Money, Money

There will be upfront costs before your actor starts generating an income. Develop a realistic budget, financial limit and timeframe for how far you're willing to go with this venture.

1. Find a bank that understands what a Coogan Account is and set one up before your actor has the first audition. Producers are required by law to put 15% of the minor actor's earnings into their Coogan Account. Your actor can take control of this money at the age of 18.
2. Get a good referral for an accountant who understands entertainment tax issues, including how to get incorporated.
3. Spend wisely and on budget. Classes, headshots, travel, dues, etc., are going to be expensive. NEVER pay for representation or auditions.
4. Get good references for everything and do your research on every person or service you are considering spending your budget on. There are people who will try to sell you things you don't need or have poor quality or reputation.
5. ALL of your actor's earnings belong to them and should be deposited into a separate bank account.

More Money Tips:

- Before there is any income, keep a list of deductible expenses you advance for your actor's career. When there is income, give the list to your accountant to consider as a reimbursable start up loan. If approved, a percentage of your actor's earnings can be used over time to pay back the loan. (Optional)
- When your actor is making enough income, business expenses can be deducted from their own earnings.
- Some parents take a salary to pay for their job as CEO of their actor's business. *Consult your accountant* to learn how to legally set yourself up as an employee and discuss a fair pay rate. Alternatively, you could hire a business manager to handle things at this point.
- Younger actors don't need to know exactly how much money they are making. They should be acting for the love of acting, not the income.
- Don't rob your actor of learning the value of a dollar. Give them an allowance or let them get a part-time job that won't interfere with audition hours.

Mistakes In Payments Are Not Uncommon:

- Get copies of all contracts so you know exactly what payments to be expecting.
- Create a system for keeping track of the Coogan deductions on the pay stubs and match them with the Coogan Bank Statements of Deposits.

Tip #8
The Balancing Act

Life as a parent of a child actor is a constant balancing act between:

1. The amount of attention given to your actor *and* your other children *and* your partner *and* yourself.
2. The time you invest in your actor's career *and* the time needed to invest in the interests of their siblings.
3. The actor's life *and* "normal" life.
4. Being a parent *and* being your actor's business manager.
5. Not being a "stage parent" *and* legitimately looking out for your child.
6. Keeping them in an age appropriate world *and* acting roles that can expose them to life issues ahead of their time.
7. Being available for any job opportunity that might arise *and* needed time off.
8. Your own career *and* theirs.
9. School work *and* auditions.
10. Your actor's body image *and* what the entertainment industry promotes.
11. Making big decisions for the good of their career *and* letting them make some decisions for themselves.
12. Keeping your family values intact *and* letting your actor step outside those boundaries to accept a coveted role.

Tips For The Tightrope:

- Well-rounded actors have more job opportunities. Let them explore things in life outside of performing.
- Your behavior serves as a model to your actor on how to handle the ups and downs in this business and in life. Keep a good balance by not making a huge fanfare for the wins and not being too disappointed when the wind blows the other way.
- In addition to time on set, there are interviews, wardrobe fittings, publicity events, etc., requiring your time. However, the dance recitals or ball games of siblings must receive the same weight. Take turns with your partner so your time can be shared with all children equally.
- Don't put your life on hold while sitting on sets. Ask the PA (Production Assistant) for the Wi-Fi code so you can work remotely, start an online business, learn a language, etc.… Your kids will fare better if you have a life too.
- Don't forget your adult life. Have date nights and socialize with your friends on topics other than your children.
- Make sure your kids know you love them for who they are, not what they do. Don't make every conversation you have with them be about the business.
- There are roles for all body types. Keep them clean and healthy. That's it.

Tip #9
Staying Ahead of the Game

This business is a hurry-up-and-wait kind of thing. You'll need to think ahead because anything can happen at a moment's notice OR you'll need to wait for something to happen… seemingly forever. Be prepared for both.

1. Keep your stress to yourself. Your actor has enough to worry about just learning lines, getting into character, and walking into a room of strangers whose personalities are unpredictable.
2. Leave with extra time to spare; traffic and parking can be tough. Your actor needs time to go to the bathroom, take a deep breath, and review the material before walking into an audition or job.
3. Always have multiple childcare options available for siblings in case of last minute auditions or bookings.
4. Keep a separate "set bag" stocked and packed ahead of time. Your actor might get hungry, tired or bored, so be ready at all times! They will need to rely on your positive attitude and your bag of goodies!
5. Prepare your actor for the possibility that their part could end up on the cutting room floor, especially with smaller roles.

Preparation Mitigates Stress...

...making each audition or job more of an exciting, new adventure. Your actor will do their best work if relaxed and in a positive state.

- Before any audition or job, map the location to see what the place looks like and figure out the parking options. Get a traffic app for your phone.
- What to keep stocked in your car depends on the age of your actor, but in general: Spare audition clothes, extra headshots and resumes, snacks, toys, nap items, music that wakes them up and gets them energized, extra hair accessories, safety pins, stain remover stick, meter money, lap desk, book light and homework tools.
- A set bag can include much of the above, but pack separately so it's an easy grab and carry. Include copies of work papers (i.e. Coogan info and Work Permit).
- Childcare arrangements are crucial. Don't thrust siblings onto strangers at the last minute. Be prepared with sitters they know and trust. Don't take siblings to auditions or jobs unless you're stuck.
- Create some rituals with your actor for auditions and jobs to get them focused, positive and feeling good. A moment of gratitude for the opportunity, your family, and your actor's team, etc..., before you get out of the car, is a great practice.

Tip #10
Just...Don't

Here are just a few things for the "Don't" list.

Auditions:
1. Don't negate the value of auditions. They are a huge part of the job. Teach your actor to be as excited to audition as they are to work. It's a chance to perform!
2. Don't put your ear to the door of an audition room to hear your actor. (I've seen this happen).
3. Don't touch anything on the Casting Director Assistant's desk or ask them questions about the audition. Text your team if you need help.
4. Resist the urge to get chatty with others inside the audition room. It's not for socializing and you'll distract the actors.
5. Don't run lines with your child in front of others, find a private place to do it.
6. Don't pressure your child for details after an audition. It doesn't matter who else was there, who went in first and for how long. Give them time to absorb the experience and later ask if there were any notes (for their coach).
7. Don't reinvent the wheel every time you need to self-tape an audition. Have a system and checklist for the process.

In General:

- Don't trust anyone to take your actor far enough away from you that you can't see or hear them. Even if they have to go inside a room without you, make it obvious that you're right outside.
- Don't make your actor always be "on."
- Don't describe your child to others as an "actor." You will be setting them up to struggle with who they *are* if they decide they no longer want to act.
- Your actor is doing something not all kids get to do and people will be excited to hear about it. Keep it casual and brief, though, and then shift the subject.
- Relax and have fun! It's an exciting business once you get the hang of it.

On Set:

- Don't get into power struggles, bribe, threaten or discipline your actor on set. Choices and distractions are always your best tools. Discuss their behavior later.
- Don't complain to anyone on set. If you have a problem, speak to an AD or set teacher out of your actor's presence.
- Don't hover, but if you see your young actor is struggling during a shoot, either with their lines, directions, or for a personal reason, it's time to be alert. Don't interrupt the director, but let the studio teacher know your child might need a moment. They will know how to be most helpful.

Tip #11
"The Mom" / "The Dad"

In this business, you are referred to as "The Mom" or "The Dad." Embrace the title knowing you're a vital part of your actor's team.

1. You manage the business income and expenses; arrive on time to auditions, jobs, coaching and classes all over the place; and keep your actor "work ready" at all times (i.e., help with lines, prep for interviews and events, have the right clothes, keep them cleaned up, etc…).
2. On set, you keep them as happy, well rested and as stress free as possible. You look for signs that they're getting tired, hungry, bored, losing focus, have to pee, are about to cry or start a fit, and you discreetly take care of these things before they become a problem for production.
3. You motivate and nurture, praise without spoiling, and teach them to show respect for every single person on set and off.
4. You know better than anyone when your actor isn't doing their best and how to help them get to that place.
5. You stay out of the way, while keeping a parental eye, and pop up seemingly out of nowhere as soon as you are needed.

If you are demanding, overbearing, entitled, or inflexible (and modeling that for your actor), you will get labeled as a "stage parent."

Here Are Some Ways To Avoid That Title:

- Show everyone from the start that you are helpful, cooperative and easy to work with, while keeping a watchful eye on your actor.
- Know when to be the parent and when to step back and let your actor do their job with the professionals they work with.
- Do your best to stay out of the way of the production, but find a spot where you can still see your child on a monitor. Always make sure the set teacher and AD know where you are in case your actor needs you between shots.
- You have every right to be with your actor in wardrobe, hair and makeup, and everywhere else. However, these people have demands on their time to get their jobs done so don't distract them. Let your actor develop rapport with them.
- If your actor is young, create a bit of sign language with them so they can communicate to you from the set if they need something. This teaches them to make choices about when to ask for help.
- As your actor gets older, foster their independence and skills to handle themselves as a professional without you on set. Gradually step away for longer periods at a time.

Tip #12
Kids Will Be Kids

This business can place a lot of demands on your actor at a young age. Keep an eye on their emotions and let them know they can tell you anything without judgment or guilt.

1. What kind of thoughts and feelings does your actor have after an audition? Are they energized and positive, capable of handling the notes, capable of moving on with the day, happy to tell you about how it went? Or are they sullen, moody, tearful, doubting, angry, or unable to let it go, even if they did a good job?
2. How about the personal demands of being an actor? Are they devastated by last minute cancellations of playdates or missed birthday parties and sleepovers? Or do they get over their disappointment after awhile and get excited for the opportunity that has arisen?
3. When they are preparing for auditions and jobs, are they motivated and focused? Or do they get easily frustrated, defensive, cry or say they can't do it?
4. Is there any particular time in the process from auditioning, to booking a job, to being on set, that you notice unusual anxiety or acting out?

Managing Stress

Negative or stressed out behaviors don't necessarily mean your actor wants to quit. It's a demanding job so give them some room for all kinds of emotions. However, if they do want to quit, they might be afraid to tell you. They may also feel that if they quit, they are failures.

- Make sure they know you will support them if they need a break or decide they don't want to act anymore.
- Teach them what to expect every step of the way. Understanding what is going to happen before it happens can relieve anxiety and disappointments.
- Acknowledge their frustrations so they feel heard, but speak positively and normalize the stressful experiences.
- Ask yourself if you could be contributing to their issues unintentionally. Do they see you stressing, complaining or looking bored? Are you too controlling or too critical? Are you putting pressure on them to succeed or subtly contributing to their feelings of guilt if they don't?
- Teach them that everything is a win. If they didn't book a role, they got in front of a CD and showed their stuff. If they didn't perform as well as they wanted to, they learned what not to do next time.
- If things get stressful for whatever reason, try and find the humor. Make a game out of it. Goof around when you can, get silly, create rituals and make special memories out of it.

Tip #13
Fame

When you make a big deal out of celebrities you teach your actor that if they become successful, then people should treat them differently too.

1. Watch for changes in your actor's personality, both in and out of work settings. If you don't like what you're seeing, don't wait to have a conversation about keeping true to themselves.
2. If someone starts fawning all over your actor, model for them how to respond graciously, grounded and real. Teach them to be humble and appreciative.
3. There is no harm in letting your actor enjoy the limelight now and then on special occasions. They deserve to be recognized and celebrated for their accomplishments. Just bring them home and get back to real life when it's over.
4. Teach your actor to appreciate the hard work of others to foster their perspective of being a *team player* as opposed to a *star*. Thanking the hair and make-up staff after touch ups and picking up in their dressing room at the end of the day are examples to consider.
5. If they have a lead or a series regular role, show them how they can make a guest star or day player feel welcome.

Interviews

- Never grant an interview without the team's input first to make sure it's legitimate. Teach your actor interviewing skills, including good etiquette and what to do if they don't know how to answer a question.

Gifts

- Have a plan for how you're going to handle gifts from fans, productions or fellow cast members ahead of time. They are not uncommon to actors, and siblings are likely to get jealous.

Media

- Do NOT let your actor open their own fan mail. They may receive some very inappropriate communications. Your actor's maturity level should dictate how you handle their fan mail in general.
- Your contact information for your actor should never be your home address. Protect their name and image on all forms of media. Consider a PO Box.
- Be vigilant regarding your actor's social media practices. Have guidelines for what you allow your actor to post of themselves on all platforms.
- Look at photos of the Fanning sisters or the Sprouse twins when they were young. They are a good example of how to dress your actors so that they are not sexualized at a young age.

Tip #14
Behaviors on Set

The most effective discipline comes in the form of natural consequences. This is tricky when your child is an actor because you can't hold the business hostage just to teach them a lesson.

1. Practice catching them behaving well. When they handle themselves professionally, are gracious and respectful, cooperative and focus on their responsibilities, etc., point out how proud you are to see it.
2. A young actor may not have an interest getting to know everyone they work with. You can still teach them about the process and what others are doing around them so that they have more context for their experience. This will prevent them from focusing only on themselves.
3. If it's too late to stop a behavior, don't discipline them on the spot. Apologize on behalf of your actor, if they are young, and then take them aside as soon as you can to discuss what happened.
4. Never talk negatively about the business or anyone in it around your actor. The more positive you are about the people and the opportunities, the more your actor will want to behave in an exemplary way.

Unruly Child Actors…

…rarely get past the audition stage. CD's are good at sensing which children don't have the right temperament for the work. However, that doesn't mean your actor won't have some less than admirable moments on set.

- When you are on a set, always assume someone can hear you, no matter where you are. Choose your words wisely.
- Instead of reprimanding for misbehavior, try to solve what your actor might be needing that is causing them to act out. Are they tired, hungry, upset about something, scared or anxious? Solve that problem first, so that the work can continue, and discuss with them later any problems the misbehavior caused.
- Threats and bribes are not useful. Choices and natural consequences will serve you both better.
- Power struggles are often a sign your older actor wants more independence. That doesn't mean you remove any guidance when needed. Respectfully let them know if they are making choices that could jeopardize their career.
- Guilt trips are toxic and will backfire. They only exacerbate poor behavior. How hard you're working and whatever you are giving up to afford your actor this opportunity is your decision as an adult. Focus on finding the root of their misbehavior instead.

Tip #15
On Their Own

Helping to transition your actor into their own career is not difficult, especially if you've been increasing their responsibilities as they've grown. Go slowly and only add one task at a time until it's mastered. Some actors might embrace it, while others might stress out. Follow their lead and gauge what they can handle. If they mess up, show them how to fix it without stressing about it. Here are a few things you can get them started with as they grow.

1. Auditions: Manage their schedule, research who they're meeting with, know the tone of the project, learn their sides, set up coaching, choose audition outfits and write them down for callbacks, keep a log of audition information, feedback and shoot dates, know how to sign in, keep headshot and resume updated, have back up clothes, know the parking situation, and call the team if late.
2. Booked Job: Required paperwork to start the job, school materials organized, how to get there, reading a Call Sheet, learning their lines, rules of the set and how to get around, knowing who is in charge, packing a set bag, when to call their team, and *writing* thank you notes.

Give Your Actor A Task

Watch them do it, give them feedback, let them know when they've mastered it, and then hand it over as their ongoing responsibility.

- Start this process early and your actor will get more pleasure out of their work because they will take ownership of it.
- If they're young, start simple, like signing in at their audition, or hanging up their wardrobe after a shoot.
- Always keep their safety in mind when handing them responsibilities. Remember they are children in an adult business.
- When they get their driver's license, don't rush to let them drive to auditions and jobs on their own. Traffic is stressful.
- Sixteen is a good age to let them start communicating directly with their team instead of through you. Continue to be copied on emails for awhile until you can see that they are handling their appointments properly.
- In their late teens, I recommend you still go to set the first day or two of a job. Once you have a good sense of who they are working with and how safe the location is, etc., let them do their thing!

Congratulations! You've nurtured your child's passion and helped them to develop an exciting career. They've learned many lessons, had some great experiences and developed important skills that can apply to whatever they do in life. Bravo!

You've finished. Before you go…

Tweet/share that you finished this book.

Please star rate this book.

Reviews are solid gold to writers. Please take a few minutes to give us some itty bitty feedback.

ABOUT THE AUTHOR

When Lima Bergmann's fourteen year old daughter, Lyndsy, asked if she could take a modeling class for the summer, Lima had no problem saying yes. One thing led to another and eighteen months later, Lyndsy was offered a three-year contract on the CBS soap opera, *The Young and the Restless*. Lima and her husband were surprised to be in the position of having to decide whether to quit their jobs, sell their house and relocate to Los Angeles or spend a lifetime wondering how things might have turned out for their daughter.

What followed were fifteen years of home schooling, auditions, acting, dance and singing lessons, meetings with agents and managers, and many hours of sitting on sets for both of her daughters. Between both Lyndsy and her younger sister, Hannah, they have worked over a hundred jobs in commercials, theater, film and television.

As a clinical psychologist, Dr. Bergmann spent the first half of her career treating children and families in foster care, juvenile hall, and as the Clinical Director at a mental health clinic in the San Francisco Bay Area. After moving to Los Angeles she transitioned to a private practice specializing in counseling entertainment industry clients. In addition to her therapy practice, Lima offers private consultations for families who are navigating the entertainment industry with their child actors.

As a speaker, Dr. Bergmann addresses audiences on the issues facing families in the entertainment industry, including the differences between supporting and sabotaging their child's career.

To contact Dr. Bergmann for private consultations, speaking events or interviews send your request to
DrLima@RaisingChildActors.com

If you enjoyed this Amazing Itty Bitty® Book
You might also enjoy…

Your Amazing Itty Bitty® Communicating With Your Teen Book – Christine Alisa, MS

Your Amazing Itty Bitty® Parenting Teens Book – Gretchen E. Downey

Your Amazing Itty Bitty® Family Leadership Book – Jacqueline T. D. Huynh

And many other Amazing Itty Bitty® Books available online.

www.ingramcontent.com/pod-product-compliance
Lightning Source LLC
Chambersburg PA
CBHW061304040426
42444CB00010B/2519